How To Promote Your Book

The importance of knowing your audience and your key message

Diane M. Hinds

The Entertainment Bureau Ltd

Copyright © Diane M. Hinds 2016

All rights reserved, including the right to reproduce this book, or portions thereof in any form. No part of this text may be reproduced, transmitted, downloaded, decompiled, reverse engineered, or stored, in any form or introduced into any information storage and retrieval system, in any form or by any means, whether electronic or mechanical without the express written permission of the author.

The right of Diane M. Hinds has been identified as the writer and author of this work, has been asserted by her in accordance with the Copyright, Designs and Patents Act of 1988, and any other subsequent amendments thereto.

The views expressed in this work are solely those of the author and do not necessarily reflect the views of the publisher, and the publisher hereby disclaims any responsibility for them.

ISBN: 978-1-326-80657-6

PublishNation
www.publishnation.co.uk

Contents

Introduction

About This Book

Chapter 1	1
Research	2
Chapter 2	8
Promotional Tools	8
Organisation	8
Press Release	9
ISBN	12
Website / Blog	13
Social Media	14
Photographs / Images	16
Product Price	17
Launch Date	18
Book / Product	22
Chapter 3	23
Techniques of Persuasion	23
Chapter 4	26
Building Your Database	26
Updates and Final Checks	26

Chapter 5	31
Press Release Distribution	31
Making Contact	31
E-mailing	31
Personalise Your Email Content	32
Follow-up	32
Chapter 6	34
Interviewing	34
Always Be At Your Best	34
Chapter 7	37
Media Coverage	37
Assessment and Analysis	37
Chapter 8	40
Extending the Campaign	40
And finally ...	41
Credits	43

Introduction

Diane M. Hinds is an experienced PR who has devised for clients campaigns across the arts and entertainment sector,  these include promoting fiction and non-fiction titles. At age 48, she felt she was losing her edge due to the increasing influence of the Internet, so she decided to go to university to study Public Relations. A woman who thrives on personal engagement, she felt cut off from contact with media personnel, and forced to work with new technologies that the younger generation handled with ease. Where she once telephoned a journalist to pitch a story she now had to present a formal pitch and chase people via channels of communication; gateways where more often than not, there was no response. The frustration of not knowing why a story was not being picked up led her to believe that a new modus operandi was required.

Diane felt that the university course leaders would laugh at her during her interview, but her application was accepted. Diane, an avid student, was excited by Audience Studies, News &

Public Opinion, and Media Transformations. She approached her course leader, hoping to explore these subjects further and was advised to transfer to a Masters programme. Cultural studies fascinated her and she pursued this field of study.

Diane met the friend of one of her writer clients, Anne Perry. They developed a friendship, despite Diane living in London and Victoria in San Francisco. Victoria teaches courses in Creative Non Fiction at UCLA Extension Writers' Programme and invited Diane to be a guest visitor in the course. This marked Diane's launch into online teaching of PR techniques.

As her Master's degree course continued, Diane bumped into the course leader of the BA Public Relations course in a cafe in Hampstead. She was invited to present a campaign to students in the first year of the course, and was later asked to co-teach the Campaigning & Persuasive Skills module. This changed the course of Diane's life, and she is forever grateful to the lovely Trish Evans, an extra-ordinary, clever Course Leader, responsible for making the University of Westminster's *BA: Public Relations & Advertising* course (newly named), the UK's number one PR course of 2015 and 2016, according to the Guardian League Table.

About this book

In 2015 Diane devised two talks and a one-day workshop aimed at literary festivals and libraries. The talks are 'An Introduction To Public Relations' and 'How To Promote Your Book' and the workshop, aimed at businesses, is 'Getting Your Message Across'. This is an interactive workshop which looks at research, defining the target audience and interviewing technique, which is available to "mumpreneurs", home businesses, start-ups, Small, Medium Enterprises (SMEs) and more.

Her interactive presentations have been held primarily at libraries. Among the favourites is 'How To Promote Your Book'. By the end of 2016, Diane will have presented over sixty talks and workshops. This book aims to help those seeking to promote themselves, and to serve as an introduction to running a successful campaign.

Chapter 1

I appreciate that as a PR, and particularly a member of an older generation, that I did not grow up with a strong sense of narcissism. Like me, you may pre-date the Internet, and that is not necessarily a bad thing. However, as I often reiterate in my talks and workshops, we live in a DIY era, a 'do-it-yourself' time in which the Internet enables our efforts. Look at video bloggers (vloggers) like Zoella or other prominent vloggers, who have embraced all that the Internet and social media have to offer. Quite unashamedly allowing them to break new ground and increase their income.

If you are thinking of self-publishing, you need to put aside all feelings of narcissism. Yes, with certain tools and information, you can promote yourself and your book, and you need to undertake this with gusto and determination. You cannot be timid or reserved, you have a book to promote and sell. This is how you raise awareness of yourself as author, but also your book. Here is the preliminary work that needs to be done.

Research

Where do you start? Ask yourself, what is your book about? Is it historical mystery, contemporary crime, humour, diet book, self-help, children's story? Have you done your research to define your target audience? Can you describe your target audience? Who are they? What is their demographic and classification? By this I refer to our social grade definitions - ABC1: Upper middle class, lower middle class, skilled workers, unskilled workers and so on. All of this is very important because you need to know exactly who will buy your book. It will also help you to refine your key message and determine which media will reach your audience, knowing this.

Some people of different backgrounds and nationalities will fit into several demographic groupings. What is their income bracket likely to be and where do they shop? How do they get information about what books interest them? You need to research your target market using the same methodologies that you use to research your book.

What media outlet does your target audience use, newspapers or online? Do they watch television or obtain their information through the Internet? If so, which sites? YouTube, Vevo, CNN, Fox, Sky, BBC News are all possibilities to explore.

To find out about my favourite actors, singers and bands, I record (on my satellite provider's box) chat programmes such as *The Jimmy Fallon Show*, *The Ellen DeGeneres Show* and *The Graham Norton Show*. In the UK, the channels on mainstream television airing chat shows have reduced in recent years, hence the need for me to rely on satellite. I also like to watch the American formats because they are predominantly nightly.

Don't get me wrong, *The Graham Norton Show* and *The Jonathan Ross Show* (amongst others) are great entertainment, but each has a shorter, less frequent run in comparison to some of the American equivalents. I'm not intentionally promoting cultural imperialism, but the UK has limited terrestrial outlets (again, in comparison to the US). This is how I find out what's going on in the wider world of entertainment.

I must also mention magazine programmes that appear on television, especially those featuring health/medical items, cooking, fashion, as well as the entertainment found in guest interviews. Don't we all need occasional entertainment to see who is doing what, and where they are doing it? It's also a way for me to learn which upcoming show will feature which actor or actress, or when a singer is going to release the next album. I'm an entertainment PR, so these programmes interest me greatly.

So what about this process of research? It's time consuming, to be sure, but there's nothing like doing the ground work to give you a strong foundation on which to build and promote your brand. Once that's established, you need to consider your media outlets.

How do you determine media outlets best suited to your project? Look at your target audience and you will determine very quickly the types of media outlets they require. Once you've done this, you will have to research the media audience. For this, I recommend you gather a database of media contacts. These can be found via an Internet search. It takes time, but it's valuable data for your project.

An excellent source of information is the traditional newspaper. What is its political leaning? What is the daily circulation and price? This is important if you wish to consider trying to lead the news agenda with your book PR, if you have newsworthy research to support it, for example.

Start by identifying the literary or books editor at the national media. By 'national media' I mean those media that cover the United Kingdom, or the country where you live. Which daily newspapers cover most of the UK? My list includes The Times, The Daily Mail, The Daily Mirror, The Daily Telegraph, and more. It also includes national television programmes such as This Morning and Good Morning Britain (ITV), BBC Breakfast (BBC 1), Newsnight (BBC2), and more. On radio, I look to The Today Show and Loose Ends (both on BBC Radio 4), The Steve Wright Show (BBC Radio 2), and TalkSport, as opposed to local media.

After you've made your list of traditional national media, research their online editorial teams. Again, find out the name of the features editors and their contact information. If you can't find an email address, you can also search for them using your preferred search engine, for additional information, if it's available.

Where possible buy the daily paper and see which editorial features (columns, guest articles, etc.) invite writers to submit their work in consideration of that editorial. There are newspaper sections (such as *The Mail On Sunday, You Magazine*'s 'Spotlight' feature, etc.) that may be receptive, for example, to up-and-coming writers with a fashion slant. Perhaps you could pitch a worthy interview contender for consideration of the *Financial Times* 'Lunch With The FT'? There are many editorial pieces which are 'celebrity' led. Your job is to research what is available and where. In order to stay current, I suggest you update your media database at least every three months.

It would also be beneficial to consider writing a feature article relating to your book, and then seeing if the media outlet you contact may be interested in featuring it. This will depend largely on the subject of your piece. For example, do you have new research regarding education, and proof that your ideas work? Can you write a minimum of 500 words about it? If you answer yes to both questions, your next step is to research the identity of the education editor or writer. When that's achieved, then you pitch your article. If you are successful, be sure to have the appropriate images, if required, to accompany the commissioned article.

What happens if your work results in an offer to publish your piece? You might be offered a fee. However, do not be disheartened if you are not. Many print outlets, including online, don't pay, and you must remind yourself that paid or unpaid, you have the value of being published. We'll delve into this later.*

Chapter 2

Promotional Tools

Organisation

What do I mean by Promotional Tools? These are what you need when you're rolling out your campaign:

- Press release!
- ISBN (International Standard Book Number, required for all published books)
- Website - Your company or personal website/blog. If you are traditionally published, include the publisher's website, too.
- Social Media sites - Twitter, Facebook, Instagram (to name a few).
- Photographs/Images – author (called a Head Shot), reference images, pictures of prepared dishes for a cook book, landscapes and points of interest for a travel book, poses for a fitness book, etc.
- Product Price
- Release date - Yes, this is *very* important (when determining the media plan).

- Book – Whether hardback, paperback, or digital.

Press Release

The most important tool in your campaign! This document introduces you and your book to key editors in the media.

Your release will contain all necessary information, including your all-important message. How do you create this message?

- Start with a blank piece of paper, or your computer word processing document, and centre the book title.
- Under the title, centre your name.
- Write a paragraph that describes the book. Keep it short, concise, compelling! Include how it relates to the news agenda, if at all. The first three paragraphs are key to introducing the subject matter to media personnel. Follow this with one punchy paragraph about the author.
- A section titled 'Notes for Editors' should be added. This is one short paragraph that gives vital important information not covered in your email body. This information needs to be bite-sized details, using a

bullet-point format. Keep your points to no more than five, if possible.

- Create a new heading, **Links**. This section delivers all of your social media links, including your web or blog site. Below that, add your ISBN, price and release date, again as bullet-points.
- To bring everything together, add your boilerplate information. This is simply 'For review copies, interview requests and more, contact John Smith by calling 123 456 7890, or email at contact@mydomain.com.' You want to make yourself easy to contact! It is important that you do no 'waffle.' That is, stick to the key information and facts, which will help you engage with your media reader.

Ideally, all this information is contained in a one-page document, and certainly no more than two. I've worked with press releases that are longer, but only because the tour information exceeded sixty dates and, when promoting a tour, all dates of appearance, venue and venue details must be included. If you're pitching an event, the ticket price per venue is different, so you will need to add that or include the mention that ticket prices vary. If you're promoting a tour, all relevant date information must be included in that one press release.

Where possible, it would be helpful to add quotes from reviews, or quotes you have received that relate to you and the book, particularly if they are from famous or influential people. These are called testimonials, and they carry a lot of weight.

When you compile your press release, it is very useful to read it out loud to yourself. This always helps to catch errors, unnecessary words, and generally improve its tone. Get someone you trust to listen, and then read it, so you'll be told where improvements can be made. If you are in a writing group, pass it around to see if they can help improve it. Believe me, as a fast-touch typist (last recorded at 96wpm), I cannot proof my own writing!

When you are happy with this press release draft, add it to your email document. As a pointer, I tend to add the date of the release in the email's subject panel: *12 December 2022 - Diane Hinds to release her debut guide 'How To Promote Your Book'*.

ISBN

I advise most of you to incorporate an ISBN inside and on the back of your book. This code identifies the book as yours and contains information regarding who published this particular edition, and other information, if the book was edited by more than one person. It also enables stores to order your book from distributors (who make the book available for events as well), and for the general public to buy. If you go into a book store or order online, you can just key the ISBN in. If it is registered with the store, it may call up all the information about that book, including the book cover.

It also helps stores know what quantity of the book they have in stock. If you request it at your library, it will also confirm if it is available either physically or digitally. A book without an ISBN is less likely to be sold by most brick-and-mortar and online bookstores.

I discovered a valuable element about the ISBN when doing my MA. I do not enjoy referencing, but it's important when writing your essays or your thesis. I used the app zotero.org to reference my books. I only had to key in the ISBN to see all the relevant information. This app also inserted the information where I required it to be recorded as a footnote, and it listed the books in the bibliography. The stress and time I normally expended making sure I had all the important information logged in, in the style the university required, was minimised greatly.

Note: You cannot reuse an ISBN, even if it's the same book. If you are fortunate to secure a traditional publisher after you've received your ISBN, they will use a different number. If you are going through the self-published route, you may not need to use an ISBN, but I do recommend it. It could save confusion, contract problems, and a headache later on.

Website/Blog

I recommend that all writers, especially those considering self-publishing, have a website. It is rare in this age not to have an online presence, particularly for the younger generation who are more likely to use the Internet as the go-to place for research.

What about a blog? Yes, you can use your personal blog, even if you are selling yourself through a leading publishing site, or dealing directly with a distributor. In any case, you need to add their website information.

Social Media

If you have not done so already, sign up for social media accounts. My two major sites are Facebook and Twitter. Depending on the subject of your work, you might also consider Instagram, Pinterest, and other sites known for images and flash (six-second) videos. If you need help with setting these up, ask your local library. They are often keen to help, especially if you do not have a computer at home.

What is the true benefit of social media? It becomes your tool for immediately reaching your horizontal network of family, friends, and potential agents, publishers, and readers. If you publish something of interest to a family member, they can repost it on their own site, which means it's viewed by their friends and followers. You never know who may end up following you, which means increased exposure.

Remember, social media is a <u>must</u> if you're a singer/band, as it allows your fans and followers to engage with you directly. If you have news to share, or 'get it here first' posts to make, social media helps to engage with them in a more personal and direct manner.

Use social media intelligently. We are well passed the basic posts of what we had for breakfast! See how you can lock into the news agenda and follow or, even better, lead the agenda and/or the debate.

Social media is also an excellent way to connect with people you admire and respect, who share your views. Follow them. It costs nothing to set up your social media presence, but the pay-off could be invaluable.

How do you join the social media revolution? You will be asked to create your profile, which is little more than sharing interesting points about yourself, and you add a picture. A good head shot is very important on social media, so think about a professional-type author portrait. If people know what you look like, they can more successfully engage with you. Avoid adding your personal contact details: they can reach you through your website or social media outlets. Never post your private phone number. And remember that personal data posted online can stay there indefinitely, even after you have removed or changed them.

Social media is quite clever these days. For example, through Facebook people can message you, if you have given them permission to follow you. With Twitter, people can Direct Message (DM) you, if they are following you. Please make sure you read through the site's policy and T&Cs first, so that you understand exactly to what you're signing up.

Photographs / Images

A hi-res image of both the book jacket and your headshot are vital, and they must be saved as a digital file. The media likes to use images to reference editorial work, and to identify you in features. You'll also need these images to promote and sell your book. A young woman attended one of my talks, and said she had written a diet book. She included before and after photos, representing the weight loss, and this helped promote her book. In Scotland, a young man spoke to me about a culinary book he was hoping to produce and I urged him to think seriously about using quality images of completed dishes that he intended to feature.

You must think seriously about images. If possible, invest in a good photographer with experience. And remember to give photo credits for all images used.

Family snapshots don't work, unless done by a pro. You want a clear shot of your face, not a plant growing out of the top of your head! Whether you're smiling or giving a 'moody' expression, be certain it represents who you are.

Any image you use in your self-published book is likely to be in the public domain for a long time; the last thing you want is to regret your choice of photos. So get this head shot sorted before you start your campaign.

Product Price

Here I reference 'product' to cover anything from books, to albums, to a cupcake business or dieting service. My basic principles apply to nearly everything that needs to be promoted to the public via media.

Do you know the retail price of your book? If you're going through third-party distribution, have you discussed the price or percentage they will pay you?

Remember that the wholesale rate is very different from the retail price. Your price can vary, but when promoting your book to the media, you need to have the full retail price. For example, if you are selling your book for £9.99, you need to add this figure to your press release.

If you are selling directly to your target audience, you might wish to consider using an online coupon site that offers a discount. However, do not forget to mention this in your press release. It could be a good 'teaser' in your campaign.

Launch Date

This is your release date, the date when your book becomes available to the general public. Most people don't realise how very important this launch/release date can be.

When I give my talks and ask self-published authors to tell me the time lapse between completing their book and making it available to sell either physically or digitally, I'm often told 'four days' or 'two weeks'. When I ask how they expect to devise a considered campaign to promote it, I get blank stares. That's when I deliver the information they need to know: Every book, when being promoted, needs to be introduced to the public. Which magazines are best for book reviews or special features? Would you contact a sports magazine about your gardening book? Of course not! But too many self-published authors skip this vital step...and lose precious publicity.

My follow-up question is often, "What's the final date for submission for the next issue of that magazine or newspaper or website?" More blank stares. My rule of thumb? Work with a minimum of a three-month lead time. For specific deadlines, go to the Submissions page (online) and you'll find everything you need.

You cannot imagine the frustration that comes with a client bringing me in one month before a UK project to generate quality coverage. That short-term lead drastically limits my ability to make contacts, and limits their options regarding media coverage. As a result, my campaign is constricted and their project receives minimal attention.

Working with this three-month lead time, I recommend you research national magazines, many of which have an editorial page featuring the contact names of those handling submissions.

If no email address is given, ring the publication and ask for the name of the literary editor, books editor, or features editor, and do not forget to update your database of contacts.

Sometimes you may get through to someone helpful, but this is not the time to pitch, unless you make contact with your key person and they express an interest. More than ever before, they will ask you to email them, but do not be put off. Respect their requests. They receive up to thousands of submissions every month. Being aggressive or offensive could lose you valuable editorial exposure.

As previously mentioned, you need to consider your release date. I recommend a minimum of a three-month lead time to cover as many media outlets as possible. I base this on traditional media (I refer to traditional media as it validates online media), and it is a great guideline for you to follow.

Consider using these lead times for specific media outlets:

- National monthly magazines — minimum three-month lead time.
- National press supplements and Sunday papers — six-week lead time
- National press — four-week lead time
- Local media — radio television and print — two-week lead time.

I am not excluding social media, but I urge you to do your research for specific online outlets that may vary from traditional media. By using the guidelines above, you'll know when to approach online outlets.

What if there are extenuating circumstances that affect your release date? A turkey farmer attended one of my talks and knew the key periods needed to focus, when it came to selling turkeys: Christmas, Easter and Thanksgiving (because of the large number of American nationals residing and working in the United Kingdom). She was also considering other times to promote her goods believing that turkey could be consumed year-round.

What if you're producing an album of original Christmas songs? Would it make sense to promote this to coincide with Valentine's Day? I think you get my drift: always think about a minimum of a three-month lead time.

Book / Product

I haven't forgotten about that book you are promoting! By now, you should have your manuscript nearly completed, if not a final draft. Now you know how to sell it, possibly have distribution onboard, if required, and make it known throughout the social media!

Chapter 3

Techniques of Persuasion

Nearly all campaigns use one or more persuasions techniques when addressing/pitching their project. It is important that you understand which techniques you are using and why. Here are some you might employ:

- Argument
- Reason
- Persuasion
- Repetition
- Reputation
- Information
- Education
- Entertainment
- Fear
- Threat
- Law
- Punishment
- Pressure
- Hope

In order to promote this pocket-sized *how-to* book, I will take you through some of the techniques I'm using to rollout my PR campaign. Remember that my goal is to persuade people to buy the book!

This book is called *How to Promote Your Book: The Importance Of Knowing Your Audience And Your Key Message.* When writing my press release, I will look at utilising the most convincing techniques, such as education, entertainment, information, persuasion, and possibly hope. What else do you think I can use?

Consider a major political campaign which has impacted you. Can you determine which of the above techniques have been the most persuasive? If you chose fear, ask yourself what has been said to sway vote? If it's a well-organised campaign, you can be sure they will also use reason, threat, education, pressure…and more.

Let us consider the ALS Ice Bucket challenge from several years ago. Which techniques do you think they were using, considering this campaign began online? The aim of the campaign was to challenge one person to pour a bucket of ice water over themselves or another person. Brilliant! Why? Because it first created a sense of pressure…The pressure of the nominated individual to carry it out. And it was also entertainment.

There was the repetitious element, through others getting involved, and the participant's reputation was at stake. If challenged, people were likely to participate, subject to the level of their celebrity - celebrity therefore attracting mainstream coverage. Imagine if someone refused!

Videos had to be posted online as proof of participation. This is a great example of a successful viral campaign, which generated extensive traditional, or 'above-the-line' media coverage…for free! And participants were credited with being good sports and generating enormous donations for ALS research. This campaign succeeded because it was entertaining, persuasive, challenging, repetitious, and it tugged on people's emotions.

Chapter 4

Building your Database

Updates and final checks

I am revisiting media here, as I wish to further expand on defining your media contacts. It is most important that you put together a list of contacts under their categories I outlined earlier as per national monthly magazines, newspaper supplements, etc. Some of them may overlap, but you are preparing to roll out your campaign and you need to understand whom to contact and why.

Let us consider what is local to you. Where do you live? Find out who your local media are: radio, television and print. Again, I'm using traditional media as a basis from which to start and familiarise yourself with personnel.

Do your research to find out who the news editor is at each outlet. Do they have a specific literary or books editor? Does your local radio station have a magazine format show where they interview local guests? If so, who presents and produces it?

You will need the producer's contact information or the presenters. Your first point of contact, if you do not know the presenter, is via the producer. Get their contact details and find out when they work or are based in the office. Who in the media outlet shares similar interests to you and may be interested in your book and/or subject matter? Build your database!

In 2014, OfCom announced over 20 'community' television licences here in the UK. These channels are interested in quality local content. Research them by going to the OfCom website to see who they are and if there is one local to you. I refer to these digital channels as the tertiary network. We have national television (primary) then regional with regard to BBC and ITV local stations (secondary) and digital community channels as tertiary. Unless you have something of significant interest you are unlikely to attract primary or secondary television interest at this stage. I am not dismissing it altogether, but you need to work your way up, unless you have something of particular significance that can open primary contact doors.

One of the benefits of these community channels is that they are digital and when they post the show in which you may have been interviewed, this may go online. You can then get the online link to add to the updated version of your press release. BBC local radio also includes a lot of its radio shows online for up to 30 days to 'listen again' and you can obtain a link to the show on which you were interviewed, post it on your online platforms for your network to listen to and add to your revised Press Release. Look at other local radios that may be available as an outlet for you and your book.

Regional print is increasingly going online in order to meet demand and adapt with the times. My first port of call is to find out if there is a local traditional newspaper and mine the contact details for my news editors, feature editors, literary editors. Again, I have often found that I only need to send one press release for any editorial I have generated for it to appear online, for the same media outlet, as well.

If you are time poor, trying to deliver your campaign by going through the traditional media outlet could help, especially where media includes online editorial. This is what I call the 'two for one' approach. For your local media I suggest you work with a minimum of a two week lead time to send your press release and follow up to see if they could be interested.

If you are invited for an interview with your local television or radio station, please make the effort to attend it in person rather than give a telephone interview. It makes such a difference, particularly if you have a sparkling personality, as it shows how you come across. Do not forget, we need the audience to engage with you, follow you and hopefully buy the book you are promoting or attend the event at which you may be speaking. It also helps to make a lasting, positive, impression with the production team and interviewer — all part of building your brand.

In the course of promoting my literary festival and library appearances for my talks, predominantly 'How To Promote Your Book' I am running an on-going PR campaign to promote each talk.

The Rhiwbina Library in Cardiff invited me to give my talk. So, about two weeks before the event, I approached all the local relevant media in Wales and around Cardiff. I was very lucky to be offered an interview with the lovely Wynne Evans who had recently started his week day morning show on BBC Radio Wales. I was also in discussion with madeincardiff.tv who were interested to have me guest on The Lowdown. BBC Radio Cardiff invited me to give the interview by telephone but I offered to come in, in person and do the interview the week before the library event. It also meant that I could tell madeincardiff.tv that will be in the area the week before and secured both opportunities. I had to travel to Cardiff from London, but it was one of my best radio interviews and television interviews.

The travel costs are also tax deductible as it is part of the requirement of promoting myself and the business. Since I have been so willing, I have generated a lot of media coverage and it is helping to build my own brand. Up to this point, I do not have a book to promote, so if I can generate my own PR, imagine what you, a writer with a book to promote, can achieve?

Chapter 5

Press Release Distribution

Making Contact

Try to avoid distributing your press release as a newsletter as it can be impersonal. A lot of email clients can detect when you use certain applications for mass distribution and can divert it to junk, spam or clutter folders, away from immediate eyes.

Editors are used to being sent press releases, but please learn to respect their boundaries; do not bombard them.

Your email should now also include the book jacket and author image, or a link to a DropBox or other cloud storage facility where they can download the image, digital book, associated pictures and more.

Emailing

When you are ready to send your press release, in the subject matter of your email, add the release date first followed by the book title and author information. That helps editors decide what is urgent or not. They can then allocate that email to a particular folder to consider nearer the time.

Do not use capital letters throughout the subject matter, or use symbols that are not part of the wording, as the email could be considered spam and then trashed. Check your email name too. If you are using something different that does not look like a professional email address, that may cause the email to be automatically added to the junk or spam folder. Keep your email address simple.

Personalise Your Email Content

I think it is much nicer to receive correspondence sent for my attention rather than feel I am one of many others to receive the email, I tend to take more notice of it if it reads personally addressed to me, such as Dear Ms Hinds or Dear Diane.

Follow Up

Once you have completed the distribution of your press release, I would allow about two to three days before I follow up. I do this by calling to speak to my contact to find out if they have received the press release. If they are willing, they will ask you about the information, when you sent it, and through which email address, in order to search for it on their computer. At this point, if I have been lucky to speak directly with the editor, I have the press release ready to send again, and do so, when they are searching for it, amongst hundreds of other email addresses.

It will arrive for a second time at the top of their emails and they should be able to see it and say they have got it. Do bear in mind that some systems are slower, and it may take longer for the email to go through cyberspace. If received, the editor may ask you to give them more time to read through it, if it is of potential interest, or tell you there and then it is not for them. Do not be afraid to ask why they feel it is not suitable. You must always be prepared to learn from your experiences. If you are rejected, do not take this personally. Editors have so many things going on and a lot of work to sift through. Try and think what could you do to better engage them and 'win.'

Chapter 6

Interviewing

Always be at your best

If you have been invited to be interviewed, always accept it, where possible. Find out what the theme of the show is and ask how long is the interview likely to be. Even if you are given about six minutes on-air time, it goes very quickly. So, you need to prepare your message; what is it? If you do not know, you really need to consider what this is. Ideally it should be dominant in your press release.

Write down your top three key messages you wish to get across and focus on them. These are also known as you 'key pings'. There will be a number of good interviewers out there, but occasionally there is one who could intentionally throw you by asking a question out of left field. Try and politely bring the subject back to what it is you are promoting.

You cannot rely on the interviewer to draw out the key points for you. They will ask you questions about you or the book, but it will be down to you to get your message across. Do not be forceful, be polite and do not forget to listen. The purpose of an interview is, ideally, for the interviewer to get the information across to their audience. You are the guest on the show, and it is about entertainment and education. A 'give and take' process of question and answer. The most important thing to consider is that the interview process should be fun!

It is easy to get nervous before an interview. Think about calming techniques which you can employ to help you to relax. I breathe in deeply then release it slowly, to help calm my nerves.

If you are being interviewed on radio, you can get away with wearing anything, within reason. You do not want to turn up in hair rollers or wearing your pyjamas. Dress to empower yourself; if you feel good, you will look good and sound good. If you are being interviewed for print, think about how you wish to dress and what impression you wish to give. Some newspapers like to take their own photographs to have on file, so be prepared.

When on television, avoid wearing checks, stripes or busy print clothing. These can cause a strobing effect on-camera. With HD cameras, they can pick up quite a lot, so make sure you do not have any spinach between your teeth! Unfortunately, they say the camera adds 10lbs, so another reason to consider something appropriate to wear — a smart jacket can do wonders.

Try not to take big swathes of paper in with you, which contain all your notes, but a small, smart piece of paper which contains your prompts, if you have too. Ideally this interview should come from memory. Make sure that you physically turn off your phone, do not just place it on mute or silence mode.

Avoid wearing bracelets or tapping the table, particularly in a radio interview situation, or anywhere there is a microphone in close proximity that could affect the recording.

You will probably be told to observe the red light in a studio environment. This means that the studio is 'live' and what you say could be broadcast. Familiarise yourself with the studio and host. Do your research!

Chapter 7

Media Coverage

Assessment and Analysis

Once you have allocated a couple of days between email distribution to follow up, you should hopefully have some success. Please do not be afraid of picking up the telephone to the editors. You may not be able to get through to some, so feel free to resend the press release in case it did not get through the first time: be polite but persistent.

I work my way through the media contacts until I have made contact with them all. If I get a 'no,' I will leave it for the time being and consider how best to improve my approach to them, for next time.

Once you have distributed your press release to key media, I advise the next thing you do is to set up a Google Alert to do with your name and book title. You can set it to alert you anytime you or your book is mentioned on the Internet. It will tell you where it was mentioned and provide a link to that content. It is a very handy tool to have, and most importantly, free.

There are some companies which provide similar press cutting services, but it is costly, so unless you can afford it, start with Google Alerts. There may well be other, similar services online free to use, so do your own research.

So, hopefully you are now getting editorial coverage. Have a look at the newspaper's rate card, or online advertising rates, to compare what the equivalent in advertising coverage would cost you.

The chances are that you are looking at hundreds of pounds if you have had significant print coverage. Air time costs too. See if you can obtain rate cards for the radio station, if commercial radio, or television outlet. See how much money you may have saved yourself by running a considered PR campaign for yourself.

*As referred to earlier, PR is a better investment than advertising for several reasons. First, it is free, especially if you are doing it yourself. It may cost you with regard to telephone calls and travel, but not in advertising spend. Secondly, that free editorial gives you 'third party validation,' whereas advertising does not. PR also gives you creditability but you can't necessarily control the message.

Chapter 8

Extending the Campaign

As a writer, there are good opportunities available to you through talks. Consider the libraries throughout the country - A fantastic centre of the community! A number of libraries are looking for interesting speakers to give talks at their libraries or as part of their literary events they run, so once again, do your research.

In order to secure over 60 talks for myself and 'How To Promote Your Book' and my other talks, I researched libraries in the main cities throughout the UK and found out who organised the events.

In much the same way as delivering my PR campaign, I organised a campaign to target libraries and literary festivals for my talks. Most were interested, hence devoting 2016 to rolling out the talks.

Not many libraries pay, but that is not the demotivating factor for me. I am on a mission to do as many talks as I can. The most important thing for me is securing the date.

About three weeks before the talk, I draft the press release to send, which contains my message: 'Diane Hinds is on a mission. A mission to help empower the aspiring, small or self published writer'. That helped garner interest from the venues and then the media.

And finally

This pocket size book is an introduction to running a PR campaign for yourself. If I can generate media coverage for many of my talks, as a speaker, think what could be possible for you as a writer?

Please feel free to follow me on social media. On Twitter, you can reach me: @Diane_Hinds or @EnterBureau, or connect with me on Facebook where I also have a group 'How To Promote Your Book' where you can post questions to me and where I will occasionally add tips. Feel free to share your own tips here for fellow writers too.

Good luck with it and I look forward to meeting up with you on my travels.

Credits

Editor - Victoria Zackheim

Aaron Willis, Words by Willis Ltd (Copy-editing)

Edward Taylor, Digital Flow Ltd (Author photograph)

Neil Gibbons (Support and encouragement)

Trish Evans (A remarkable woman)

Lenore Hinds - (Unfathomable support)

Libraries and Literary Festivals that have invited me to speak, especially Sarah Smith at Brent Libraries who had the courage and conviction to invite me in the first place.

The Entertainment Bureau Ltd
www.TheEntertainmentBureau.co.uk

www.ingramcontent.com/pod-product-compliance
Lightning Source LLC
Chambersburg PA
CBHW072258170526
45158CB00003BA/1103